STONE AGE GEOMETRY
LINES

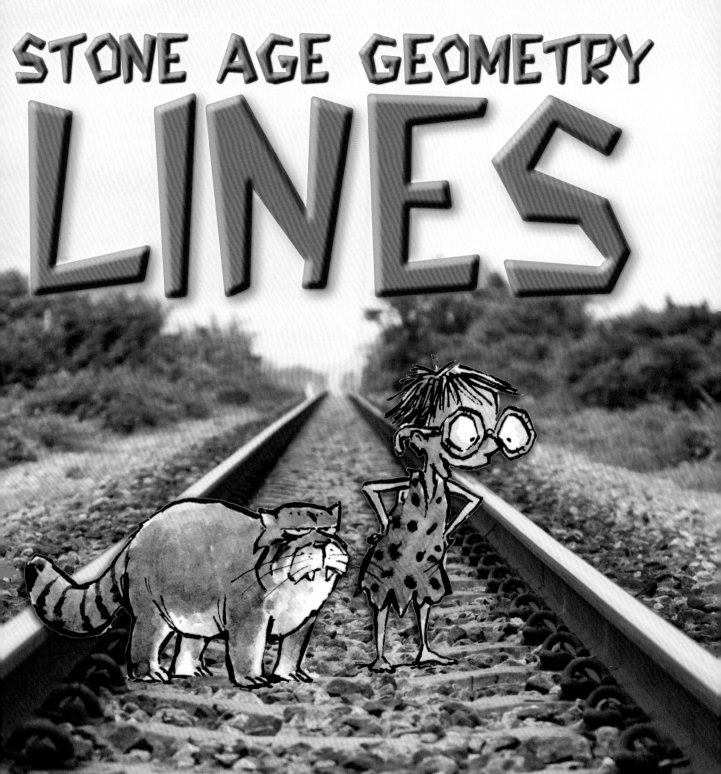

Gerry Bailey & Felicia Law
Illustrated by
Mike Phillips

Crabtree Publishing Company
www.crabtreebooks.com
1-800-387-7650

Published in Canada
616 Welland Ave.
St. Catharines, ON
L2M 5V6

Published in the United States
PMB 59051, 350 Fifth Ave.
59th Floor,
New York, NY 10118

Printed in Canada/032014/MA20140124

Authors: Gerry Bailey & Felicia Law
Illustrator: Mike Phillips
Editor: Kathy Middleton
Proofreader: Anastasia Suen
End matter: Kylie Korneluk
**Production coordinator and
   Prepress technician:** Samara Parent
Print coordinator: Margaret Amy Salter

Copyright © 2012 BrambleKids Ltd.

Photographs:

cover - siwasasil Title pg - siwasasil pg 2 - Gerard Lacz / age fotostock / Superstock pg 3 - David M. Schrader pg 5 – (t)Perry Correll / Shutterstock.com (b)Tom Fakle pg 7 - simonalvinge pg 9 – (t) Kurt and Rosalia Scholz / Superstock (m)Robnroll (b)photolinc pg 11 – (t)Patrick Wang (bl)southmind (br)Calvin Chan / Shutterstock.com pg 12 - Protasov A&N pg 13 – (t) NASA (b) MarcelClemens pg 15 – (t)MarcelClemens (m)auremar (b)Fpoint pg 17 – (tl)Fpoint (tr)Yuriy Kulyk (bl)5ciska76 (br) JNT Visual pg 19 – (l)William Allum (r)Ana Gram pg 21 – (tl)Leo Blanchette (tr) Anton Kozlovsky (ml) Jenny Leonard (mr)Photosani (b)alexxl pg 23 – (t) Nicholas Piccillo (b)siwasasil (r)viphotos pg 25 – (t) David Redondo (m)auremar (b)Picsfive pg 27 - Barry Blackburn pg 28 – From l-r clockwise Micha Klootwijk,Kodda, Peter Sobolev, Phillip Marais, MarkMirror pg 29 – From l-r clockwise alexokokok, Marco Uliana, Flegere, Henk Vrieselaar,Alekcey, Le Do pg 31 – (t) 67075645(m) flas100 (inset middle) Hellen Sergeyeva (b)Photononstop / SuperStock

All images are Shutterstock.com unless otherwise stated

Library and Archives Canada Cataloguing in Publication

Bailey, Gerry, author
     Stone age geometry: lines / Gerry Bailey, Felicia Law ; illustrator: Mike Phillips.

(Stone age geometry)
Includes index.
Issued in print and electronic formats.
ISBN 978-0-7787-0509-3 (bound).--ISBN 978-0-7787-0515-4 (pbk.).--ISBN 978-1-4271-8234-0 (html).--ISBN 978-1-4271-9004-8 (pdf)

     1. Line geometry--Juvenile literature. 2. Geometry--Juvenile literature. I. Law, Felicia, author II. Phillips, Mike, 1961-, illustrator III. Title.

QA608.B35 2014   j516'.183   C2014-900422-2
                                           C2014-900423-0

Library of Congress Cataloging-in-Publication Data

Bailey, Gerry, author.
 Stone age geometry: lines / Gerry Bailey & Felicia Law ; illustrated by Mike Phillips.
     pages cm. -- (Stone age geometry)
  Audience: Ages 10-13.
  Includes index.
 ISBN 978-0-7787-0509-3 (reinforced library binding : alk. paper) -- ISBN 978-0-7787-0515-4 (pbk. : alk. paper) -- ISBN 978-1-4271-8234-0 (electronic html : alk. paper) -- ISBN 978-1-4271-9004-8 (electronic pdf : alk. paper)
 1. Line geometry--Juvenile literature. 2. Geometry--Juvenile literature. I. Law, Felicia, author. II. Phillips, Mike, 1961- illustrator. III. Title. IV. Title: Lines.

 QA482.B3436 2014
 516.183--dc23
                                           2014002079

LEO'S LESSONS:

MEET LEO

Meet Leo,
the brightest kid
on the block.

So that's Leo!

Bright, as in IQ
off the scale;
inventive, as in
Leonardo da Vinci
inventive; and
way, way ahead
of his time....

Block, as in
Stone Age block;
Stone Age, as in
30,000 years ago.

Then there's Pallas—
Leo's pet.

Pallas is wild, and he's OK with
being called Stone Age, too; after all,
his ancestors have been around for
millions of years. That's more than
you can say for Leo's! You won't
see many Pallas cats around today,
unless you happen to be visiting the
icy, cold wasteland of Arctic Siberia
(at the top of Russia).

POINT TO POINT

"I'm going on a hike," says Leo.
"A hike where?" asks Pallas. "And why aren't I coming?"
"I have to do it alone," says Leo. "See the map?
I have to get from point A—which is right here—
to point B. If I do, I get my Scout's cross-country
mapping badge."

"Wow!" says Pallas. "A badge!"

"The shortest route between
two points is a straight line,"
explains Leo, "so that's the
way I'll go.

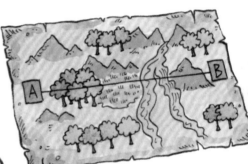

I'll have to cut a path
through the forest, wade
through the marsh, swim
across the river, sail over
the rapids, hike over the
mountain, and climb
down the cliff..."

"All that...just for a badge?"
asks Pallas. "Is it a gold badge?"

"It"s a Scout badge," says Leo,
"to sew on my shirt and wear
with pride!"

"Not gold then," sighs Pallas.
"Not even silver."

Steeple to steeple

A special kind of horse race, known as a steeplechase, is also referred to as a "point to point." The first steeplechase race took place more than 250 years ago between two villages in Ireland called Buttevant and Doneraile.

The idea to race from "**steeple** to steeple" or point to point began when one man challenged his neighbor to race from the church in one village to the church in the next. This meant galloping about four and a half miles (7.2 km) across the countryside. Both riders kept the steeple of the church in sight and aimed straight for the finishing point. They jumped stone walls, ditches, and hedges—anything in their way!

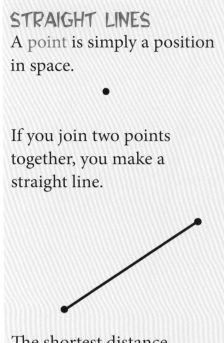

A modern "point to point" race, or steeplechase, is run on a racecourse, not across the countryside.

Two thousand years ago, the Romans were famous for building roads. Roman roads crisscrossed Europe in straight lines, going from one settlement to another. Many are still used today.

5

LINES THAT END

"Pick up the end of that rope," says Leo. "Now pull!"

"What?" asks Pallas. "You want *me* to pull?"
"Yes, pull!" cries Leo. "I want to know if you are stronger than me. I'll pull this end, and you pull that end. If the knot tied in the middle of the rope crosses the red line onto my side, I win."

"And if it crosses onto my side, I win!" says Pallas.

Leo wins.

And wins again.
And keeps on winning....

... until Pallas
gets help!

LINE SEGMENTS

A line segment has a beginning point and an end point. Line segments do not have arrows on either end.

Line segments can be joined together to make shapes. Each of the three sides in this triangle is a line segment.

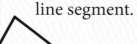

To dance the limbo, dancers must go under the pole without knocking it down. The pole forms a line segment between the two people holding it.

A clothesline, stretched between two poles, is also a line segment. It has a beginning and an end.

Worms have bodies that are divided into many small segments, which look like tiny rings joined together.

7

LINE UP!

Leo asks Pallas to stand in a line.
"Where?" asks Pallas. "Next to the big guy, or the one with the teeth?"
"Anywhere will do," says Leo. "It's a lineup.
Someone just stole my sausages. I saw them sneaking off.
I'm going to try to pick the thief out of the line."

"It wasn't me," says Pallas.
"Or me," says the woolly mammoth quickly.
"Innocent!" cries the cave lion.
"I was with my mom," says the giant beaver.
"I was with him," says the bison.

Pallas walks up and down the line.
All the animals try to look innocent.
Especially the one who is guilty!

HORIZONTAL LINES

A horizontal line is one that stretches from one side across to another.

A line is made when points are lined up side by side.

● ● ● ●

We also make a line when we stand one behind the other in a row.

A row of guards on parade outside the royal palace in London, England.

*Baby ducks follow their mother in a straight line by **instinct**.*

These children form straight rows when they exercise together.

ON THE HORIZON

"So, that line way out there where the sky touches the land is called a horizon?" says Pallas. "Can we go see it?"

"It's a long way away," says Leo. "It's as far as you and I can see. And anyway, we'd never get there."

"Why?" says Pallas. "We could at least walk to the tree over there. We'd be able to see it better."

"Pallas," says Leo. "Try to concentrate. The horizon is always as far as you can see, so no matter where you stand, you can never actually reach it."

The moon's horizon

*On July 20, 1969, American astronaut Neil Armstrong was the first person to stand on the surface of the moon. The moon is smaller than Earth, so it's **curvature** is easier to see. He watched Earth come into view, rising above the moon's horizon.*

*"It's a **brilliant** surface in that sunlight. The horizon seems quite close to you because the curvature is so much more **pronounced** than here on Earth."*

The view from the Apollo 11 Command and Service Module "Columbia"

Earth's horizon is seen here from a satellite in space.

HORIZON

There are some kinds of lines that seem to keep moving, such as the horizon. It marks the farthest point that you can see before the land and the sky appear to join.

Of course, if you walk forward, the horizon line will keep moving backward. It will always mark the farthest point on Earth that you can see.

From a viewpoint of seven feet (2.1 m) above the ground, the horizon is about 3 miles (5 km) away.

From the top of a tree, the horizon is ten miles (16 km) away.

From a plane, the horizon appears nearly 250 miles (402 km) away.

UP AND DOWN

"What are you doing way up there?" asks Pallas.
"It's this **maypole**," says Leo. "I can't get it straight."
"It's very high," says Pallas, gazing up into the sky.
"It has to be," says Leo. "We tie ribbons to the top
and dance around it."
"Sounds great!" says Pallas. "But not a cat thing.
Definitely not a cat thing."

"Pallas," says Leo, "why don't you climb up this tree
and hold the top of the pole steady, while I hold it
steady at the bottom. It's got to be perfectly straight."

"THAT sounds more like a cat thing," says Pallas,
and up he climbs.

"All done!" calls Pallas. But Leo says to try again.

And again!

And again!

And again!

VERTICAL LINES

A vertical line is one that stretches up and down. It is made when points line up above each other.

These skyscrapers in the city of Beijing, China, rise up vertically.

RIGHT ANGLES

When a line rises vertically from a horizontal line, the space between them is called a right angle. In math, a right angle is represented by a small square in the corner of the two lines.

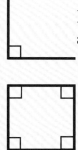

Right angles are shown at the four corners of a square.

PLUMB LINES

A plumb line is used to check to see if something is perfectly vertical. This means it must be exactly straight up and down. A plumb line is a string with a metal weight at one end. The weight hangs down from the top point of an object and points down directly toward Earth's center of gravity.

Builders use a plumb line to make sure a wall is perfectly vertical.

And ....

Barcodes are printed on the items we buy. The sets of vertical lines form an electronic code.

13

LINES AS BORDERS

"Hey!" says Leo. "Do you want to play?"
"But you're hopping around on one foot," says Pallas. "Is that playing?"
"I'm playing hopscotch," explains Leo. "I've scratched out these squares in the dirt."

Leo tosses a stone into the square marked with a 1. "Now I hop on one foot!" he says.

He hops through the numbered squares in order, skipping over the square with the stone in it. In the squares to his left, he is allowed to put his left foot down, and in the squares to his right, he is allowed to put his right foot down.

When he gets to the "safe" square at the end, he turns and hops back. He picks up his stone on the way. Next he throws it into the square marked with a 2.
Then off he goes again.

"Easy!" says Pallas and throws his stone.
"Out!" says Leo. "The stone touched a line."
"Out!" says Leo. "You hopped on a line."
"Out! says Leo. "You fell over—and you've rubbed out all the lines!"

14

LINES THAT BOX

Lines can be used to form an edge or a border.

A line can be drawn to divide something into two parts. A road is divided into two parts by a yellow line.

Lines are used on a map to show the edge, or boundary, of a country or a place.

When you draw, the line around a shape is sometimes called an outline.

Lines are drawn on maps to show the boundaries of villages and towns.

Lines can also divide an area into parts. A line painted down the center of a road divides it into left and right sides.

This huge garden maze was built in Italy.

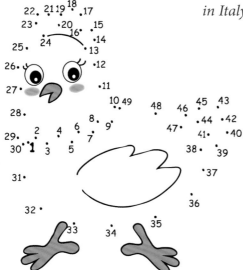

In a connect-the-dots puzzle, you draw a line from dot to dot in the correct order to reveal the outline of an animal or object.

Mazes

Garden mazes are lines of hedges grown as puzzles. The high hedges prevent people from seeing the easiest path through it. The maze becomes a test of memory and direction.

15

WHICH WAY?

"What's that?" asks Pallas. "That thing with flat branches sticking out of it?" "It's a signpost," explains Leo. "I put it there to help you find your way.

"Remember when you said you didn't know where the storeroom was?" "You wanted me to carry two heavy sacks," says Pallas. "But I lost my way."

"Remember when you said you didn't know where the quarry was?" says Leo. "You wanted me to carry two heavy rocks," says Pallas. "But I lost my way."

"Remember when you said you didn"t know where the ice pit was?" says Leo. "You wanted me to get two chocolate ice cream cones," says Pallas...

"...and I've suddenly just remembered how to get there!"

STOREROOM

QUARRY

ICE PIT

LINES THAT MEET

Sometimes, many lines all come together at one point. These are known as converging lines.

Roads that lead into the center of a city converge. The point at which several routes meet is called a junction. Drivers have the choice of going in many different directions at a junction.

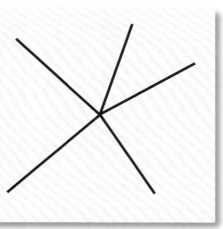

SIGNPOSTS

Signposts show the direction you must follow to get from where you are (point A) to where you want to go (point B).

Signposts often show the distance you must travel between two points.

Five roads meet, or converge, at this signpost.

The main threads of a spider web start from points outside the circle and converge in the center.

LINES THAT CROSS

Lines sometimes cross over each other. These are known as intersecting lines.

Roads intersect at a crossroads.

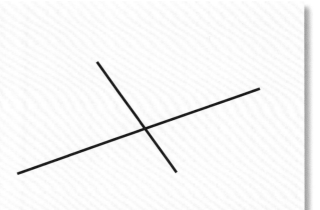

MEASURING LINES

"I'm getting taller," says Leo. "Soon I'll be tall enough to join the grown-ups in the tribe."

"Me too," says Pallas. "When I'm taller, I want to join too."

"I don't think so," says Leo. "You're not growing taller upward, Pallas. You're growing wider outward."

In fact, Leo is getting higher. Pallas is getting wider.

"Don't worry," Leo says. "Lots of animals grow in all kinds of directions."

It's true. Leo and Pallas have been tracking the woolly mammoth's growth. It has been growing higher and wider much faster than Pallas!

"Don't worry, Pallas," says Leo. "He may be taller than both of us, but they still won't let him join the tribe."

SHIP LOAD LINES

Merchant ships all have markings on their sides called load lines. These lines show how much of the ship is sitting below the water level when it is loaded with items. A loaded ship that sits too deep in the water can become unstable or even sink.

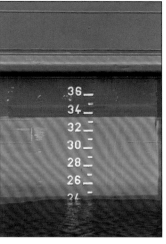

Geographers use imaginary lines drawn in a grid over the surface of the globe.

Load lines are marked on the sides of ships.

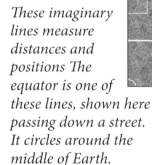

These imaginary lines measure distances and positions The equator is one of these lines, shown here passing down a street. It circles around the middle of Earth.

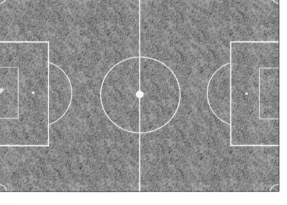

Lines marked on a soccer field show where the players can go.

MEASURING LINES

A line has length. The length of a line segment is the distance from its start point to its end point. The length of a line can be measured in units known as inches, feet, or yards (or in metric measure, centimeters or meters). Very short measurements are counted in parts of a unit. Vertical lines are measured by their height.

MEASURING INSTRUMENTS

Lines are measured using rulers or tapes which are marked out in units of equal distances.

A tape measure

SIDE BY SIDE

"Keep your feet apart!" yells Leo.
"Keep your knees apart! Keep your legs apart!

A good skier makes two lines through the snow that are nice and straight and always the same distance apart."

But Pallas is making lines that certainly aren't straight— or the same distance apart.

Pallas simply started at the top of the hill and landed at the bottom.

And he's not at all sure that skiing is a cat thing.

20

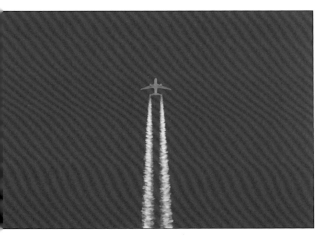

Vapor trails are parallel clouds of water droplets released from the two engines of a jet.

Parallel lines in sports

Parallel lines are used in many sports. They are usually easy to see along the sides of a field, marked on a basketball court, or as upright goalposts on a football field. They are especially important in running and swimming events where the competitors must cover exactly the same distance inside parallel lines known as lanes.

Parallel lines may sometimes appear to meet in the distance. But they never do.

The sides of a ladder are usually parallel.

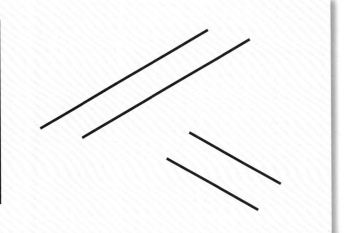

PARALLEL LINES

Parallel lines are lines that remain the same distance apart no matter how far they stretch.

Parallel lines always point in the same direction.

CRISSCROSS

Leo puts on his helmet and releases the brake.
"Look out!" he cries. "Here we go!"

Pallas clings to him on the back of the scooter. This is
a new experience, and he doesn"t feel safe at all.

They whizz backward and forward, zigzagging and
crisscrossing in one direction then another.
Each time, Leo screeches to a halt and
changes direction. Finally, he stops.

"There!" he says. "We've done it!"
"Done what?" asks Pallas.
"We've made a circle out of lots
of straight lines and no curved
ones," says Leo.

They climb up the hill to see.

Railway tracks cross over and merge, or join, at junction points so that trains can move on a diagonal from one track to another.

DIAGONAL LINES
A diagonal line runs from one corner of a shape to its opposite corner.

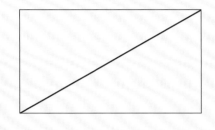

You make a diagonal line when you score in the game of tic-tac-toe.

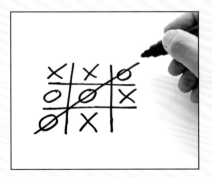

Diagonal can also describe any slanting line.

Knitting needles must cross so wool can wrap around them to make a stitch.

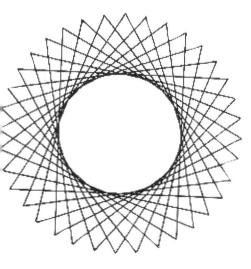

Straight or curved?
*Leo's circle looks like it was drawn with a **compass**. But it has been drawn using lots of straight, diagonal lines. No curved lines were used. Can you see how it was drawn?*

23

GOING BELOW

Pallas has a bone. He often has bones, and he usually gobbles them up just like a dog. But this is one he wants to keep for later, and he doesn't want anyone else to get it.

"Just a little deeper," he decides. "Just a little deeper to be on the safe side. After all, the cave bear has large claws."

"Maybe a bit deeper still," he decides.
"It's a good bone, and it's worth making the effort."

 So he goes on, digging deeper and deeper below the surface.

At last the bone is safely buried and Pallas can relax.

"Hey Pallas!" Leo calls. "Look what I found for you."

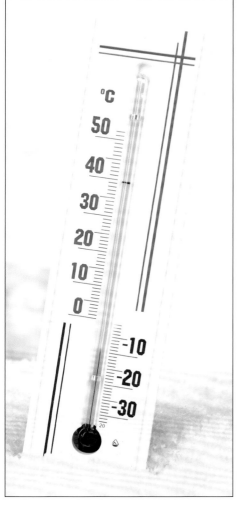

Up and down the number line

*On a **number line**, we begin counting at zero. All the numbers that are bigger than zero are called positive numbers. They are shown on the right side of zero on a number line. All the numbers that are less than zero are negative numbers. They are shown on the left side of zero.*

The temperature goes up and down on a thermometer. For example, in metric measure, negative temperatures are colder than the freezing point which is 0° Celsius.

A graph can be drawn to show how the temperature goes up and down from 3° to -3° over the 12 months of a year.

NEGATIVE NUMBERS

The number 1 is one more than zero, or 0. The numbers count upward from there: 2, 3, 4, and so on.

But numbers can count down from zero, too. These are called negative numbers. Negative numbers have the minus sign, - , in front of them. They are numbers LESS than 0. They are shown as: -1, -2, -3, and so on.

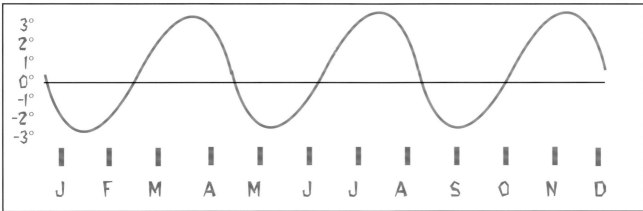

LINES IN NATURE

Nature makes its own lines. The wind and rain will carve out straight cracks and valleys in hard rocks, and make lined ripples in mud and sand. Plants use long, straight stems and veins in the leaves to carry water around the plant. Stripes in lines on the petals attract insects. Animals also use lines to attract other animals. But strong lines can also warn **predators** of danger, that the food they are hunting may have a bad taste or even be poisonous.

Lines on this cinnabar moth caterpillar warn predators of danger. It won't taste good!

Some kinds of lemurs have striped tails. These are used to recognize each other.

*Stripes can help to **camouflage** an animal, such as this zebra, against its surroundings.*

The wind can make lines across the sand. Farmers can make lines in the soil with plows.

LINE OF SYMMETRY

Many objects in nature are the same on both sides. If you drew a line down the center, and folded the two sides over each other, each side would be exactly the same. Each side is a mirror image of the other side. The line between the two halves is known as the axis of symmetry.

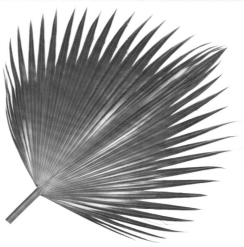

The veins on a leaf carry water from the stem to the leaves. They can also form spikes which help protect the plant.

*Bright lines on petals help attract the attention of **pollinating** insects.*

27

ANGLES

"My tent doesn't look right," says Pallas.
"It's not," says Leo. "You haven't put it up right.
In fact, I don't think you've put it up at all!

You've got to get the angle right," Leo explains.
"The sides of the tent have to make an acute angle.
Acute means sharp. Your tent is supposed to have
a sharp shape but it doesn't look sharp at all."

"Right!" says Pallas.

"However," says Leo thoughtfully, "your tent is
leaning over at a very sharp angle, so perhaps
you have made an acute angle after all."

ANGLES

An angle is the corner shape that two lines make when they meet.
The wider the two lines are, the bigger the angle between them.

A small angle

A wider angle

These kinds of angles have sharp points where they meet. They are known as acute angles.

This angle is called a right angle. You see it at the corners of pictures and tabletops.

When geese fly together in flocks, they often fly in the shape of a V or an angle.

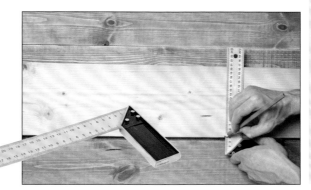

When carpenters need to saw wood at a right angle, they use a tool called a steel square.

DEGREES

The size of an angle is measured in degrees.

The sign for a degree is a small raised circle written like this: 10°.

The size of the angle is shown like this:

MEASURING THE STARS

Astronomers measure the angle between Earth and a star, or between different stars, using parts of their arms. These give very rough angles. For example, 1° is about the width of a little finger held at arm's length; 10° is about the width of a closed fist at arm's length; and 20° is about the width of the palm of a hand at arm's length.

ON AND ON

Leo is up to bat.
He swings the bat and whacks the ball high over
Pallas' head. It disappears into the distance.

"Run and get it," he tells Pallas. "If you don't, I'll score so
many points I'll win the game."
"But I don't know where it went," grumbles Pallas.

"OK," says Leo. "I'll help you even though I'm on the
other team. I hit it over there—way over there. It may be stuck
in the bushes, or it may have gone farther."

"How much farther?" asks Pallas.
"Just farther," says Leo.
"Farther than farther?" asks Pallas.
"Maybe farther than farther," Leo agrees. "What if it
went farther than that?" asks Pallas. "I mean, perhaps
it just went on and on forever, and there's no point me
looking for it ...."

MATHEMATICAL LINES
In math, a line has no
beginning and no end. You
need to imagine that it just
continues at both ends,
stretching on and on.
We show this by putting
a small arrow at
each end.

RAYS
A ray is a line that has a beginning
point but no end. We can see where
it starts but not where it ends. The
rays of the sun are like this.
They seem to stretch
away into space
forever.

LEARNING MORE

OTHER BOOKS

The Line
by Paula Bossio
Kids Can Press (2013).

Basher Science: Algebra and Geometry
by Dan Green and Simon Basher, Kingfisher (2011).

Mummy Math: An Adventure in Geometry
by Cindy Neuschwander, illustrated by Bryan Langdo.
Square Fish (2009).

The Greedy Triangle
by Marilyn Burns, illustrated by Gordon Silveria
Scholastic Paperbacks (2008).

WEBSITES

Get the facts on the line and its properties at this entertaining website:

http://www.mathsisfun.com/geometry/line.html

Find a variety of games and activities with geometry themes.

www.kidsmathgamesonline.com/geometry.html

This website provides information on shapes and their properties.

www.mathsisfun.com/geometry/index.html

KEY WORDS

In math, a line has no beginning and no end.

A line segment has a beginning point and an end point.

A ray is a line that has a beginning point but no end.

An angle is the corner shape that two lines make when they meet.

An object that is the same shape on both sides is symmetrical.

A horizontal line is one that stretches across from one side to another.

A vertical line is one that stretches up and down.

Lines that come together at one point are known as converging lines.

Lines sometimes cross over each other. These are known as intersecting lines.

Parallel lines are lines that remain the same distance apart.

31

GLOSSARY

brilliant Shining brightly

camouflage Colors or markings on an animal that hide it in its natural surroundings

compass A math tool used for drawing

circles with two pointed arms joined at the top
curvature The degree of curve of a line

instinct A natural reaction

maypole A tall pole decorated with ribbons and flowers

merchant Someone who sells something

number line A line without ends whose point are matched to real numbers by their distance away from a given point labeled zero

pollinating Transferring pollen from one plant to another

predators An animal that kills and eats other animals

pronounced Very noticeable

steeple A church tower

INDEX